The world as I know it

Jiya Jikku

BookLeaf Publishing

Presentation by *BookLeaf Publishing*

Web: www.bookleafpub.com

E-mail: info@bookleafpub.com

ISBN: 9789358731637

First edition 2023

*This book is for all the souls in this world who
are made to feel like they're not enough.*

ACKNOWLEDGEMENT

I would like to dedicate this book to all the people in my life who have made me who I am today.

I'm talking about those people who were my support through thick and thin. People like my family who've seen me at my worst and don't really have a choice but to stay. My friends who braved my battles with me when they didn't have to. The great teachers and other role models who've shaped my passions and motivated me to leave a mark on this world. All of them will be carried in my heart forever.

I'm also talking about the people so shameless I scorn them years later. Thank you for making me who I am today. You have a special place in my heart.

PREFACE

Welcome to my reality. Whether you agree with me or not, you can't deny there's some truth to all of it. Some are more pessimistic, some more hopeful. You can't cross a road while denying the bumps that leave you shaken. Like that, life isn't a smooth drive. But the view sure is great.

I hope some can speak to you when you are low and some can keep you motivated when you are on a high. Art is so fabulously versatile that way. It is the only thing that tailors to your very being at any given moment. I can't draw that well and I don't dance in public for the sake of others. But I can write well, so please grace me with your time and attention while I set my stage. Trust me it will be worth your time. My name is Jiya Elizabeth Jikku, Hello!

Parasite

As I got older,
I thought I would get bolder,
Instead I hide and cower,
On the button my fingers hover.

Guess I realized the absurdity of it all,
It couldn't have ever been a ball,
The race of life that's all it is,
And that mark I always miss.

Everyone's running constantly,
Don't they get tired?
Puppets of a monopoly,
All the way till they're retired.

Why do I feel like I'm always behind,
Too slow,
Last to cross the finish line.
I feel like I am blind,
Too weak,
To fall into that grind.

I don't know when I lost the plot,
Started feeling so distraught,
Nobody else they did halt,
All their enemies they still fought.

I keep falling behind,
So fragile is my mind,
Every mile I need a break,
Before my legs start to ache.

I was once a promising child,
Young me would be SO beguiled,
How did she flop so bad?
Lost all the hope that she had.

Now I'm such a cynic,
Guess that's what you become,
Nothing but parasitic,
Guess that's my outcome.

Only A Matter Of When

Have you ever felt
Like a nuisance to them all?
A parasite, a welt,
An uninvited guest at the ball.

I call many people my friend,
Yet in heart of hearts I believe in the end,
Nobody will stick around,
I won't hear back a sound.

They're all just tolerating me,
I'm making all their patience run thin,
I'm sure just like me they see,
All my faults and my sin.

Nobody could like that awful woman,
A parasite and a leech,
It is only but a matter of when,
Our friendship they'd impeach.

So I overthink every action,
Don't want to piss them off,
They'll throw me out of the faction,
All ties they will cut off.

I guess I'm scared of being alone again,
Like I was for many years,
I don't want to be that little girl again,
Dissented by her peers.

No Regrets

So out of place,
Wish it didn't faze,
This feels so petty,
Weighs on me heavy.

Nothing feels right,
Try as I might,
I need a change,
Time to flip the page.

Am I being ungrateful
For where I am at?
Is it disgraceful
To feel such regret?

Looking at my past,
Seeing how my mistakes last,
The way they changed so many things,
How they stole my wings?

If only I'd cared less about what they said,
Maybe it all wouldn't have got to my head,
If only I'd gotten myself out of bed,
This path differently would have led.

But what can I do now really,
So I appreciate all I have,
Love who I am now so clearly,
Look towards the bright future I will work to
have.

No regrets,
Life has its ups and downs,
As hard as it gets,
There will be laughs amongst the frowns.

Nomophobia

If I had a choice,
I wouldn't get off my laptop,
Even if it destroys,
My brain cells up top.

I get that it sounds lazy,
But please hear me out,
You might say I'm crazy,
But I have no doubt.

There are so many like me,
That's clear to see,
Slaves of the Internet,
So many I've met.

Why are we like this,
So much life we miss,
Yet we still stand by it,
The reality never does hit.

The answer is easy,
Life stays so breezy,
You can ignore the sadness,
Feel in control of this mess.

It gives you fake power,
When it's really the one in power,
A sweet addiction,
The haven's a fiction.

Yet I still won't let go,
Sometimes it's all I can rely on,
Eventually everything makes me feel low,
Except what plays on my phone.

I know it sounds strange,
Borderline derange,
But I know you relate,
If you want to change, accept your state.

The fire that keeps me running

It's a struggle,
But I won't give up,
I always fumble,
Overflow my cup.

But I get up again,
I don't have a choice,
Won't sit in this hole again,
Won't give up my joys.

It doesn't hurt to try,
How many more nights do I cry?
About the situation I'm stuck in,
A sad rotten bin.

It's not a yes or no,
I have to give my best attempt,
To get to a heaven so,
Empty of all contempt.

I know it'll never be perfect,
Flawlessness I don't expect,
But I want to trust myself for once,
Believe I'm more than a useless dunce.
So I'll work hard to be,
The absolute best version of me,
Even if the finishing line is hard to see,
I want to finally be truly free.

For that I will do anything,
The fire that keeps me running,
I'm willing to give up everything,
All these escapes so cunning.

One day I'll truly love myself,
I'm a fool if I'd say it'd be easy,
One day I won't withhold myself,
With my anxieties that make me queasy.

Heal the inner child

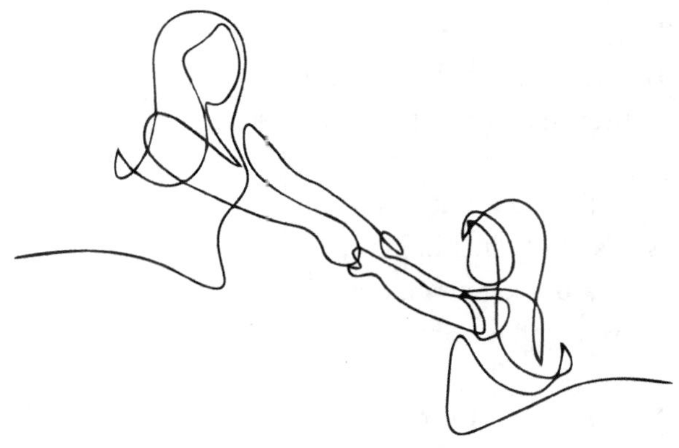

Heal the inner child,
Or she'll always hold you back,
Be the shelter where she can hide,
Give her everything you once did lack.

She was only six,
When she really needed someone,
Her mind was in a mix,
All of it was so sudden.

Can you imagine a girl so small,
Practically a baby,
Having to go alone through it all,
Having to bear it like a lady.

She deserves a hug,
A hot chocolate and a rest snug,
Give her a break,
Her heart still does ache,
Be the protector your mind would always make,
All for that poor little girl's sake.

Don't condemn her whining,
She's really just in pain,
It's hard keeping on compiling,
A facade that seems sane.

You can't run from her,
Forget who you once were,
You'll always carry her along,
So you're misery don't you prolong.

Be who you needed then,
Then again you'll feel so whole,
Back to who you were when,
Before the demons marred your soul.

The Modern Narcissist

The modern-day narcissist,
We're all guilty,
The modern-day narcissist,
This includes me.

We live off likes and follows,
No matter how much it hollows,
The wasted experiences we dedicate to,
Getting the perfect pictures that's true.

A need to prove ourselves,
To the followers on our page,
Everyday we lose ourselves,
In this pursuit of value we engage.

Consumerism has made us shallow,
A bunch of losers following fades,
Soon we'll be like land fallow,
Reflecting in our grades.

I used to be my own person,
But the pressure to fit in consumed,
Now I'm not so certain,
Who I am not costumed.

I guess we all felt,
The need to be like the rest,
Blaming ourselves for the cards we're dealt,
Settling for no version but our best.

Comparing ourselves with everyone,
Instead of cruising at our pace,
Feeling pathetic when they post their fun,
Passing life in this unsatisfied daze.
There was a time,
When the internet was not at its prime,
It was group chats and a memory guide,
Under a fake self we didn't need to hide.

Now we're a bunch of caricatures,
Not a single glimpse of truth,
When will we realize in our own way we're all
treasures,
Stop wasting every second of our youth.

Enjoy the view

In myth they speak of soulmates,
Two halves of a whole,
I think you are my soulmate,
Filled in that empty hole.

I'm an awkward mess,
But with you I must confess,
I don't feel an ounce of that usual stress,
Why that is I can't guess.

It's so pleasantly unexplainable,
The way you make me feel,
That sort of peace I thought unattainable,
Like an unbreakable seal.

I don't feel like I have to be,
Anyone but myself,
This false good in me you see,
Scared the real me you'll unshelf.

When I tell you that,
You say to me with a pat,
'You really don't see what I do,
You silly little fool.'

I don't know why I lost my trust,
Guess it's just my own protection,
I'm sorry I have a thick crust,
From the years and years of rejection

Yet you don't give up,
When I run away,
You wait for me to let up,
This useless, long chase.

That's when I knew,
Maybe I could let down my guard,
For a little while enjoy the view,
Before it all gets unbearably hard

Nothing but perfect

Her legs too long,
She's too damn strong,
I see some flab,
Where is her glam?

She's way too short,
Not really hot,
Why she so wide?
Got too much pride.

She's such a nerd,
Her head's a daze,
She got no herd,
Not much to gaze.

She's either too bossy or meek,
This chaff all they speak,
She's either too much or too little,
A bull or so brittle.

She's always judged under a microscope,
Causing her to lose all hope,
Of ever being loved as she really is,
With all of this unneeded diss.

A perfect obedient daughter,
A flawless unbending mother,
A zealous efficient worker,
A loving trophy wife.

Nothing but perfect,
Is what they expect,
She needs to remain a Mary Sue,
Trying hard with so much to do.

Break the chain

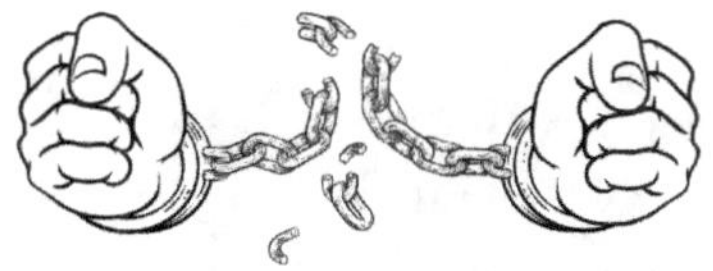

We stay away from the bane,
To prevent all that pain,
Barely staying sane,
Finding someone we can blame.

People panicking everywhere,
Birthdays ruined that's not fair,
It seems like summer just got ruined,
Everybody now so prudent.

Home seems like a prison,
The whole world in indecision,
It all seems like a pointless mission,
How did we end up in this position?

I know it seems all too overrated,
These precautions get so overheated,
Some say it's just a cold,
But there's so much we are not told.

People dying everywhere,
Some passing with no say,
Some not getting needed care,
When it's more than they can bear.

So we must play our part,
It's the least we can do,
And keep those lost in our heart,
While brave souls fight this flu.

The Power To Make The Change

We have the power to make the change,
But we put ourselves in a cage,
In front of our screens all day,
Why are we this way?

We react to all the crazes,
The Internet, a world of endless mazes,
We let our lives be wasted,
Why did we let them get tainted?

We can leave a mark on this Earth,
A footprint in the dirt,
But we'd rather see the memes,
And videos and snaps and tweets.

We could stop that terrible war,
The rape of our daughters and the pain,
The abuse that we don't face,
but others do from a cane.

We could even save a life,
A precious innocent life,
But we'd rather look away,
When we see all the wicked rotten strife.
I know Insta can be funny,
You can even get some money,
You get hearts and "friends",
The joy seems like it has no ends.

But come into the real world,
One with sorrow and hurtful words,
We have the power to make a change,
But we'd much rather escape.

We don't have another

She's slowly dying,
Earth is crying,
Her distress keeps multiplying,
But you still keep on denying.

Droughts ravage our fields,
Damaging our yields,
Tornadoes cause so much mess,
Yet you don't even stress.

People are literally dying,
Fighting hard to keep surviving,
The rich just keep on thriving,
Disasters keep on arising.

They stay blind to this ordeal,
Not seeing what it's done,
But soon they'll have to kneel,
When the damage is finally done.

There's a consequence for every action,
Every mistake has a reaction,
When will you open your eyes,
And see past all these lies?

But we can still change our fate,
Before it gets too late,
Let's save our giving Mother,
We do not have another.

Unwelcome visitor

It's hard letting go,
Of the baggage that brings woe,
Every time it knocks on my door,
Leaves my heart broken and sore.

The moment it all feels right again,
It creeps back up on me again,
'Surprise! Did you think I would leave so easy?
Life will never again be light and breezy.'

I'll stay a boulder on your back forever,
Happily ever after is a never,
Talk of growth and healing all you want,
I will always be here to haunt.

So I guess I just have to get used to it,
The unwelcome visitor that never left,
I'm just gonna let it sit,
A constant, unjust, smooth theft.

Story to write

Stand up for yourself,
What are you doing?
Stand up for yourself,
The hurdles will keep queuing.

Treat yourself,
The way you dream of being treated,
Believe in yourself,
Then others will believe you blindly seated.

Your worth is in your own eyes,
Which others peer into,
Impressions are not a rolled dice,
You decide how it ensues.

Others' opinion doesn't matter,
They don't know the full picture,
The story behind the mad hatter,
Probably was a trauma-filled mixture.

Even us we were small-minded,
Just calling him crazy,
In our own reflection we're so blinded,
Our vision turns so hazy.

So just do whatever you want,
At any given moment,
Be your own unique font,
Be your own type of potent.

Never bend down,
For those trying to bring you down,
They have their own struggles,
After all, we're all just simple muggles.

Trust me no one really cares,
So flaunt your expression,
Don't be scared of getting in their hairs,
We all just want some attention.

Trust me it's all in your head,
Stop overthinking,
Get out of your bed,
Stop spiraling and sinking.

Be the little dreamer you,
You have a world to conquer,
You have so much to do,
Nothing can make you falter.

Be a little delusional,
All the greats were,
Don't think of it all as impersonal,
Stop seeing life as a blur.
You are the main character,
You have a story to write,
Don't leave empty your calendar,
Keep reaching for the height.

Prisoner

I feel the panic building up,
The water about to tip the cup,
I feel the spiral falling falling,
Being teased by the brutal calling.

From outside you can't see the maniac,
How my mind's running round frantic,
The thousand scenarios on the silver screen,
To myself why am I so mean,
I've seen everything that could go wrong,
My excitement already lost in the throng.

So I tell those who love me I can't come,
Making up some excuses but they're not dumb,
They know what's happening they're all
annoyed,
It won't be long till they start to avoid.

I don't blame them though,
What an awful friend, daughter, sister,
Believe me I'd do the same I know,
I'm being an unwanted blister.

I just want to be the old me,
It's been so long I can barely see,

The confident, bold queen I used to be,
Why can't I just be free?

Yet I put these shackles on myself,
I have no one else to blame,
Yet I feel so powerless to myself,
A prisoner of my own brain.

Legacy To Make

We're all dependent on something,
A job, a hob, a person,
Making it our reason,
Making it our drive,
To be best at it we always strive.

I guess it's to ignore the fact,
In the end it's all so meaningless,
No matter what you use to fill the lack,
We're just a speck of dust in nothingness.

Maybe that's why we made religion,
Something to tell us what to do,
To be part of some bigger envision,
So we listen to the nonsense they spew.

Why are we put on this earth?
Made up into something from just dirt,
I want to leave a mark on this planet,
So I have to change my habit.

No more clothes thrown on my bedroom floor,
My cupboard decked up pristine.
All the plates and cups don't belong on my study
table,
To reflect on my grades my environment must
be clean.

My parents will believe in me more,
Eventually I can only hope,
See I have the ability to soar,
Be more than just a downward slope.

I have to start now,
No matter how small,
Maybe go for a little walk.
I don't know how,
How many times I'd fall,
Yet this time I'd know it's all crock.

I'll keep getting up,
I have a legacy to make,
Myself I will build up,
To something they can't shake.

I will no longer be weak,
A pushover so meak,
I believe in me,
My own worth I see.

If it's all so meaningless,
I will give it my own meaning,
Don't compromise on your happiness,
And you will always be gleaming.

Be That Person

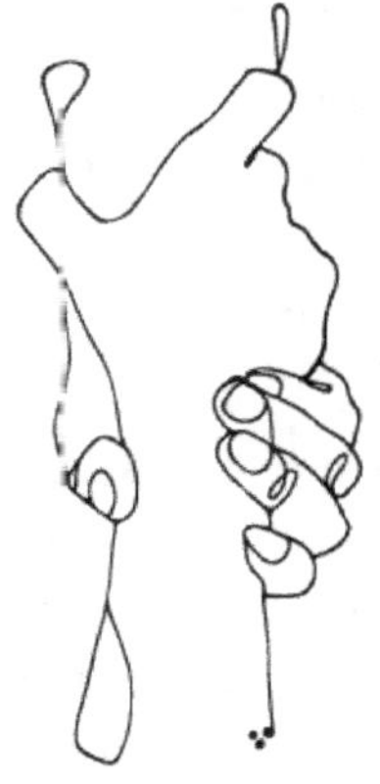

Everyone is fighting just like you,
Each have their hills to conquer,
Everyone is struggling just like you,
Just like you they falter.

We're all just human after all,
Life is not meant to be a ball,
Everyone has their own imperfections,
Our own set of beliefs and misperceptions.

Don't believe in the disdain of others,
They only see you from the eyes they were
taught,
From their youth and from their mothers,
They have their own set of thoughts.

Only see yourself through your own eyes,
And realize everyone is as confused as you,
They are going after their own prize,
They don't mean any harm to you.

Be kind to everyone,
We're all barely getting by,
Didn't you want someone by your side?
When all you wanted to do was hide.
At my lowest I was at my worst,
I acted out when I needed someone,
Just needed a hug to quench my thirst,
To be heard, To be seen by someone.

Be that person to your kin,
You could save a life,
That's what life is supposed to be about,
Be the kindest soul you see about.

Ignited

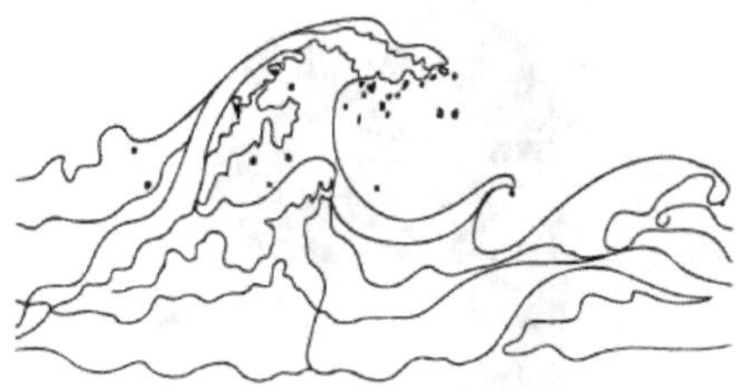

I have a whole world left to explore,
Than my little tiny world now there's more,
I have so many memories to make,
So many polaroids to take.

So many new friends to meet,
New people that inspire me,
So many new dishes to eat,
And wonderful sights to sit and see.

My life has really just begun,
Imma keep riding till the setting sun,
There is so much on my bucket list I have to get
done,
Doesn't that sound so fun!

Just the thought of it gets me excited,
Makes me want to work hard to be the future
me,
A fire in me gets ignited,
What will the future make of me.

My Cute Grandpa

*"I wanted to give this poem to my Achacha
on his 85th birthday. But just before I could,
he passed away. His presence was a treasure
to so many and I will always miss him dearly.
My greatest hope is that he's looking down
on me from above"*

My cute grandpa had a bit of a temper,
Always told us to be our all,
Make a mistake and we'd hear a lecture,
No deal in his mind was small.

He never said, "I love you",
Never hyped us up enough,
Always telling us what to do,
His love was always tough.

Yet I heard him pray for us at the breaking dawn,
Monotonous and yet a hopeful song,
Taking the name of his grandkids and kids one
by one,
He prayed may the Almighty keep us strong.

My Achacha turned out to be so cute,
Even if about his love he was mute,
Even when we irritated him more,
I know he loved us ever more.

We came home to our grandparents' place,
To Ammama's mouthwatering food on the table,
But behind the scenes stood Achacha's grace,
Making sure all of us ate from a bountiful table.

His love language was special,
Always looking out for us was Achacha,
We know he loved us on a higher level,
Never seen a gem like my grandpa.